FROM, A COUNTRY DIARY

WAYNE CLEMENTS

KFS

Newton-le-Willows

Published in the United Kingdom in 2018
by The Knives Forks And Spoons Press,
51 Pipit Avenue,
Newton-le-Willows,
Merseyside,
WA12 9RG.

ISBN 978-1-912211-22-7

Acknowledgements:

'Wenlock Edge (second)', 'Sandy (#2)', 'Oxfordshire', 'Oxfordshire (third)', and 'Hardham' were first published in *Kenya* (Veer, 2016).

These poems were written over a year, October 2015 to October 2016. Words and phrases from *The Guardian* newspaper's Country Diary series were used to create the new texts.

– Wayne Clements. November 2016.

ARTS COUNCIL ENGLAND
LOTTERY FUNDED
Supported using public funding by
ARTS COUNCIL
ENGLAND

FROM, A COUNTRY DIARY

CONTENTS

Watership Down

wet beech
  wet down
chalk down
  beech and the chalk and ash
of the ash woods
  face of woods
that north face
  that cover the steep north
cover the steep
  cover the steep
cover

Wenlock Edge

the devil
  the devil
the devil-cursing bush
  cursing the devil fell
a bramble bush
  fell from heaven
in a bramble
  from heaven
and landed
  and landed in
and landed

Sandy

for years the trees
  for years a hedge
of a hedge
  the trees had been the false impression of
had been linked by –
  giving the false impression –
linked by a chest-high mass
  branches giving a chest-high mass
of fallen branches
  of nettles and fallen nettles
brambles, brambles and brambles

Sandy (second)

brambles and fallen brambles
  and hedge no hedge
fallen branches
  no hedge
branches giving no hedge
  giving the false impression
no hedge
  the false impression of no hedge
of a hedge no hedge
  a hedge but no hedge
but lately no hedge
  lately the debris
no hedge
  the debris had no hedge
had been no hedge
  been cleared
no hedge cleared
  leaving no hedge
leaving a pronounced no hedge
  a pronounced bank
no hedge
  bank but no hedge
but no, no hedge
  no hedge
no hedge
  hedge

Wenlock Edge (second)

the hawthorn berries
  the hawthorn moon
under the harvest moon berries
  shines nights
under the harvest shines with
  and nights with bright autumn rains
and bright autumn days
  morning rains
days morning days
  morning days

now the haws
  now brown gold
brown the haws are
  at red
gold are
  at their gold red
their most yellow
  gold most dazzling
gold yellow dazzling
  though green gold
though not gold green
  not yet gold
gold yet edible
  (and is gold edible?)
and the season
  the season is the season

Oxfordshire

bonfires these bonfires
  the time is the time
these burn
  (it is burn all day)
after it all day
  and the hour
after and every day
  and the hour
every day
  but sunset
but sunset
  and but sunset

smoke drifts
  smoke disappears
countryside disappears
  drifts horizontally
the whole countryside
  horizontally over
and the whole
  over the fields
the hedges and the fields
  and through the hedges
and threads its way through
  threads its way
threads its way

trees and trees
  smoke and smoke
and mists
  mist and mists
and of mist and the planes
  of the solid
the flat planes
  solid ground itself
because the flat ground itself
  seem to –
is it because –
  seem to breathe
and skyward
  (is it breathe)
and to gaze
  to gaze skyward
to gaze

Waresley Wood

in this
  in crossover and crossover
this dense overlapping
  and dense wood
so much overlapping wood there
  and so much there
were boughs
  and were so many boughs
so many
  so many, many trees

to the dying
  to the new trunks
new dying
  to the new trunks
to the leaves, trunks, new leaves of new trunks
  of leaves with new leaves
dying trunks with dying
  log, new trunks
log full fresh
  new full of their own
fresh of log
  with their own log and fresh with
and twigs become fresh twigs
  full branches become full
and their own branches
  and thickened
become their own
  thickened and to become
and twigs

and to twigs thickened to branches
and thickened to branches thickened
to branches thickened

Tilton Cutting

an area
  of an area
oak leaves
  of oak
of shady browning leaves
  of shady damp
and browning
  damp tranquillity
goat willow and tranquillity
  overhung and goat willow
overhung now
  of ash
and now in autumn
  foliage of ash
in autumn
  with the yellowing foliage
with the yellowing
  with the yellowing

Oxfordshire (second)

cold winds
  cold to come
still to come winds
  and is still and heavy rain
is heavy rains
  more rain rains here
suggests that more
  here for summits
suggests that for the last
  the hill summits
the last day along the hill
  day or two hangs along
or two
  and that hangs
and the dim mist
  that the dim mist
the dim mist

Oxfordshire (third)

under plough
  under the stubble
over the stubble
  plough the main
in a semicircle
  over the main body
of outposts in a semicircle
  body has a scattering
of outposts
  has ranged out a scattering
ranged itself
  thrown out itself along
has thrown along the border
  and has the border
furrow in a straight line
  and furrow in a straight line
furrow in a straight line

Wenlock Edge (third)

stares into
  stares east north east
into a north east
  a field
north east field
  that north east
that opens north east
  opens under
north east
  under a north east
a mutation north east
  mutation of north east
of redwings
  north east redwings
fieldfares north east
  fieldfares and north east
and thrushes north east
  thrushes just north east
just arrived north east
  arrived from north east
from the north east
  the north
north east
  north east
north east
  east

Hawthorn Dene

woodland edges woodland
  their branches from their branches
edges and berries from
  and even strip berries
even elder
  birds strip elder blossom
while birds blossom appearing
  appearing while appearing

grow fast
  grow here
flower here fast
  and set still in flower
and set seed
  were still in seed
in several
  were in fissures with
of soil several fissures with
  minute amounts
minute amounts
  of soil
minute amounts

Henstridge

scarified and cut
  scarified and oversown
to be cut
  oversown with are to be
with a wildflower of pollen are
  a wildflower seed

the foxes deer told
  of the foxes
deer and green was told of
  green woodpeckers
and was told
  woodpeckers that frequented

Wenlock Edge (fourth)

it comes, it flowers
  ivy flowers
comes from feeding on ivy
  from the wasps feeding on the wings
and wasps
  wings of hoverflies
of hoverflies
  and of hoverflies

do as do butterflies
  tortoiseshell butterflies
as the small tortoiseshell
  the light is ragged
small light is held
  in greenbottles ragged
held in their wings
  the itinerant hoverflies
greenbottles, their wings
  like flakes that the itinerant hoverflies like
flakes of mica know that
  of mica or shreds
not know
  or shreds of cellophane
or may not
  of cellophane
they may
  they may
or may
  they may

now broken
  now the end
before the end
  broken that idea
flowers before that idea may –
  ivy flowers may –
travel
  in the ivy
travel in the dreaming
  in the, in the insect of dreaming
insect wings
  a moment of wings
in, and a moment in, their buzzing lives
  and their buzzing restless, restless lives

Hardham

a dunnock is a dunnock
  singing is singing

the South
  the sky
the sky
  South Downs
across the Downs clouds are racing
  across clouds are racing
clouds are racing
  clouds are
                across the valley
across the clouds are Downs
  clouds are
valley to the South
  to the South Downs
to the South

St Dominick

past downland
  past tall gorse
covered in tall gorse
  downland
past tall gorse
  covered in past flowers
covered in tall gorse flowers
  yellow tall gorse
covered in yellow flowers
  luminous tall gorse flowers
downland covered
  in luminous downland
hedges of tall gorse
  covered in hedges
of luminous hedges
  of tall gorse
luminous yellow
  yellow hedges of yellow

Blaid's Wood

in the briars
  in the sunset
some winter sunset
  some briars
and the winter
  and hazels
of the hazels in the corner
  in the glow of
in the corner of
  the shone in
the glow of the field
  field shone field

Vagastie

winter's solstice
  the winter's skyline
above the skyline
  solstice
the sun it grasps
  above the sun doesn't rise here
it grasps
  doesn't rise far
far here
  far

alive and dead
  alive and the living moss
the living dead damp moss
  the living damp acidic moss
the living acidic ground moss
  the living ground grows moss
the living
  grows sphagnum moss
the living sphagnum moss
  moss, the living moss
the living moss
  the living
the living

it's frozen
  it's water
thin water frozen
  but bone thin
but there is matte-like bone

  there is no translucence
it's matte-like
  no translucence
it's no translucence
  it's no translucence

Claxton

of light
  of completed things
completed light
  the aura of things
the swelling damp
  this aura of swelling damp
and in this and the quietness
  join in the quietness of the air
seem to join
  of the air after all
and season
  seem to after all
the day and season
  the brisk morning
even the day
  brisk morning
even the brisk morning
  even the brisk morning

Warblington Cemetery

grass overhead
  grass ragged like ragged overhead crows
and the air like crows and jackdaws
  through the air jackdaws wheeled
wheeled through
  wheeled

toppled and weatherworn
  toppled graves on graves
and weatherworn and wizened holly placed on
  and wizened holly berries had been placed
berries clung to the wreaths that had been
  clung to the wreaths
that clung to the wreaths
  that clung

amid the dead
  amid a blackbird and a blackbird
the dead sprang bloom
  and sprang new full bloom
new life in full
  life beside
were in beside the daffodils
  were the kissing gate daffodils

Wenlock Edge (fifth)

dark bird
  a dark marsh and marsh bird
a shower
  pools and shower
of the flood pools
  of rain over the flood
rain passes
  passes over
passes

South Uist

starlings' startles
  starlings' wings
a clatter of wings startles all
  in a clatter of all the birds into
the air in
  the birds into
the air
  the birds into the air
the birds

Westmorland

afternoon faded
  afternoon
or birds or sheep
  or birds faded away in –
or sheep or birds
  away in a wild sunset
or sheep or birds
  a wild sunset and –
or sheep or birds
  and the first –
or sheep or birds
  the first stars
or sheep or birds
  stars began –
or sheep or birds
  began to –
or sheep or birds
  to peep –
or sheep or birds
  peep out –
or sheep or birds
  out from –
or sheep or birds
  from this –
or sheep or birds
  this direction
or sheep or birds
  direction and at –
or sheep or birds
  and at this –

or sheep or birds
  this time of –
or sheep or birds
  time of day
or sheep or birds
  day with –
or sheep or birds
  with huge banks
or sheep or birds
  huge banks of –
or sheep or birds
  of cloud
or sheep or birds
  cloud building –
or sheep or birds
  building up –
or sheep or birds
  up all –
or sheep or birds
  all round
or sheep or birds
  round and –
or sheep or birds
  and not –
or sheep or birds
  not a sight –
or sheep or birds
  a sight of –
or sheep or birds

of trees
or sheep or birds
trees –
or sheep or sheep
or birds or sheep
or birds or sheep
or birds or birds

Allendale

greenery as the greenery
    the woodland
part of the woodland
   as the long dead
to become part of the long dead tree
   back to become tree

soil already soil
   leafmould the darkly wet leafmould

Kendal

the snow began
  the snow on my –
black snowflakes
  on my –
black began to fall
  to catch snowflakes
to fall
  I went out
to catch –
  I went out
I went out
  I went

away across away
  I stopped
the hill
  I stopped
across the small lane
  below the hill
the small lane
  and the fields below
and into
  into the fields

Wenlock Edge (sixth)

raven or raven
  – it, what was it?
or buzzard – what was it?
buzzard, see
  – what was it?
see it
  – what was it?
it up there
  – what was it?
up there or
  – what was it?
or did they
  – what was it?
did they only
  – what was it?
only look
  – what was it?
look down
  – what was it?
down, could
  – what was it?
could the
  – what was it?
the smaller
  – what was it?
smaller furtive
  – what was it?
furtive birds sense
  – what was it?
birds sense anything

– what was it?
anything in the
– what was it?
in the sky
– what was it?
sky
– what was what?
was it what was?
– it, what was it?

South Uist (second)

now and again
  now and then
seas and then again other seas
  and then other waves
seas and then waves
  presumably seas
and then presumably in seas
  and then in response to seas
and then response to underwater
  seas and then underwater rocks
seas and then rocks form at –
  seas and then form at right angles
seas and then right angles to the seas
  and then to the oncoming seas
and then oncoming seas
  and seas
and then seas
  and then seas
and then

Haslington Trail

and green
  and like grass
like green shoots
  the grass shoots
raindrops in the raindrops glitter
  glitter in glitter

bright yellow
  bright path
well-trodden path
  yellow flowers
well-trodden path
  flowers embroider
well-trodden path
  embroider the well-trodden path
the well-trodden
  well-trodden path
well-trodden path
  well-trodden path

Allendale (second)

of spruce
  of ferns
ivy and ferns
  spruce, larch
ivy and ferns
  larch, sycamore
ivy and ferns
  sycamore and ivy
and ferns and birch
  ivy and ferns
birch
  beneath lies –
ivy and ferns
  beneath lies a muddle
ivy and ferns
  a muddle of fallen –
ivy and ferns
  of fallen branches
ivy and ferns
  branches and ivy and ferns
and plants
  ivy and ferns
plants that –
  ivy and ferns
that jostle one –
  ivy and ferns
jostle one another
  ivy and ferns
another bramble
  ivy and ferns

bramble, dog's mercury
   ivy and ferns
dog's mercury
   ivy and ivy and ferns
ivy and ferns
   ivy and ferns
ferns

Bodinnick to Polruan

then dark
  then a rainbow
from inland a rainbow
  dark clouds encroach from inland
clouds and blasts
  rain encroach
and blasts of cold
  of cold rain
of cold

by cliffs
  by scrub
blackthorn scrub
  cliffs and in the blackthorn
and steep pastures
  sing in the steep pastures
violets, and robins sing
  violets speckle coastal path
and robins speckle turf
  by the coastal path
turf by the turf
  by the turf

South Uist (third)

were buried
  were once burned
a fire once burned
  buried and the place
a fire and fragments mark the place
  fragments of wood
mark of charred charred wood

Wayne Clements

Highland Water

they're dying
  they're living
of the living-dying flowers
  limb of the flowers
on a fallen larger limb
  on a fallen branchlet
on the larger branchlet
  on the branchlet
on the branchlet

Nene Valley

cold evening
  a cold fog and fog
evening
  a clear night comes
dawn and clear night
  and then comes dawn
and a frost
  a frost
then a frost

Wayland Wood

this is still this winter
    in winter is still a wood
locked in a wood locked
    a wood locked
a wood

twig ends
    and twig ends
rise, the trees rise
    and as the trees rise
as the trees
    the trees rise
the trees rise
    the trees rise

Ebernoe Common

the trees are the trees
  green the green
are still
  and the still bare celandines
and bare but lesser celandines
  but spring yellow
lesser spring flowers
  anemones
yellow flowers are wood anemones
  are emerging starlike
wood emerging through
  the white starlike
through the leaf litter floor
  white leaf litter of the woodland floor
of the woodland
  of the woodland

St Dominic

a chiffchaff sings
  a chiffchaff
wild and wild sings
  above the dog's mercury
and above the sunken lane of dog's mercury
  sunken lane
where bluebells –
  the green of
– where bluebells –
  stitchwort between
the green
  stitchwort and alkanet
– bloom between
  and alkanet bloom
and alkanet bloom
  and alkanet

Ribblesdale

of corals
  of strata
or formed strata
  or corals
other sea formed strata
  or other sea creatures living
formed strata
  or creatures
living and dying
  formed strata or –
and dying in formed strata
  – or in such formed strata
or such quantities
  formed strata
or quantities that piled formed strata
  or that piled skeletal formed strata
or skeletal remains
  formed strata
or remains formed
  formed strata
or formed strata
  or formed strata
or strata
  or –

Litchfield Down

here the downs
  here the flint
and flint
  downs are earth
and are a rolling sea of earth
  a rolling sea of a rolling sea of a rolling sea

the arc of a furrow
  the arc
the hill
  of the hill
of a furrow
  and disappears
the crest of
  and disappears over
over the crest

riddled and sorted
  riddled and spat
and sorted
  and spat
and sorted
  and spat
and sorted
  and spat
and spat

Wenlock Edge (seventh)

fruits and fruits
  bone, feather and bone and snails
feather and bone
  snails, leaf, feather and bone
leaf and feather and bone and twig
  feather and bone
twig made feather
  and bone made flesh
feather and bone
  flesh, feather and feather and bone
feather and bone
  feather and bone

Claxton (second)

here and there
  here it is
leaves it is
  and there with the leaves it is
with the fresh green leaves it is
  fresh green of leaves it is
of blackberry leaves it is
  blackberry leaves
leaves it is
  leaves it is
leaves it is
  it is

whitethroats may creep
  whitethroats may
they illuminate
  the weather they illuminate
creep among
  or the weather
among nettles
  as ourselves
or nettles
  but as much as ourselves
but as much
  but as much

Sinderhope

of a cuckoo
  of a repeating and repeating cuckoo
reverberating
  reverberating
and reverberating

Claxton (third)

rooks overhead
  rooks that fly
all that fly overhead
  sedge warblers, they scratch away
all sedge warblers
  mimicking as they scratch away
mimicking linnets
  the metal gate
as linnets and clanging the metal gate
  and Hereford cattle
Hereford cattle clanging
  Hereford cattle

Wenlock Edge (eighth)

of cloud
  of flash floods
stair-rods
  flash floods
cloud bursting dogs
  stair-rods bursting into tempests and dogs
into tempests
  thunder, cats and thunder
and lightning
  and lightning
cats and lightning

Sandy (third)

from the bathroom
  from the door
the back door
  bathroom
the bedroom at the back
  the bedroom
or the eaves
  at, or standing under, the eaves
standing under
  standing under
standing

Drakewalls

now bright
  now trees are birch trees
are bright with the lady's mantle
  birch with the summery purples
and lady's mantle
  summery purples of fleabane
and of selfheal
  vetch, fleabane, selfheal, thistle
with yellow vetch, thistle, buddleia
  interspersed with yellow
buddleia, rosebay and knapweed
  interspersed
rosebay and knapweed
  rosebay and knapweed
rosebay

Backstone Bank

woodland gone
  woodland and wood sorrel
and gone were the primroses, wood sorrel
  were the songs, sanicle, primroses
songs of woodruff, sanicle
  of wood, of woodruff
wood warblers
  flowers of warblers
and of spring flowers and blackcaps
  the carpet of spring
blackcaps gone too
  gone too the carpet
gone too

Airedale

over my head
  over my exhausted
– look –
  exhausted head
a jay always
  – look, a jay takes flight
in flight
  always takes flight
from the sycamore
  but jays in flight
from the sycamore
  as the bird exhausted
but jays
  – as the bird crosses
and exhausted crosses
  the winged and the river
heavy winged
  river to the
– it looks heavy
  to the meadow beyond
it looks meadow and hawthorns
  and hawthorns beyond and hawthorns

Hill End

of fescues
  of the dog violet
the fescues
  eyebright
late blooming dog violet
  eyebright
selfheal
  a late blooming selfheal
tormentil and even a tormentil
  and even tormentil
and even tormentil

rain will wash away rain
  will be over
  will be over
wash away their spoil
  in the sun will
their spoil heaps
  few weeks
in the sun heaps
  and their few weeks
and all trace will disappear
  their all trace
of them
of them
  will disappear
of them

Surrey

the west and the west
  the robin
branches
  the robin
and south branches
  the robin
south and branches
  the robin
and rich branches
  the robin rich green branches
the robin
  green underneath
branches
  the robin
underneath a few branches
  the robin
a few butterflies
  branches
the robin
  butterflies alight
branches
  the robin alight on them
branches
  the robin on them
finches
  branches
the robin
  finches and branches
the robin and a robin
  branches

the robin
  a robin
perch on branches
  the robin
perch on the branches
  the robin
the branches
  branches
the robin
  branches
the robin
  branches
the robin
  the robin

Wenlock Edge (ninth)

unclear its unclear eye
  dark eye
its deep, deep dark deep

www.ingramcontent.com/pod-product-compliance
Lightning Source LLC
Chambersburg PA
CBHW051703040426
42446CB00009B/1270
* 9 7 8 1 9 1 2 2 1 1 2 2 7 *